The Soul of a Man

A testimony to rising out of darkness
to find faith and one's true calling

Colin Jones

Diamond Legacies
your story is your legacy

Editor & Book Designer:
Cheryl Antao-Xavier
cherylxavier2022@gmail.com

Published by:
Diamond Legacies
inourwords2008@gmail.com

ISBN: 978-1-989403-41-9

Dedication

I dedicate this book, *The Soul of a Man* first and foremost to God, my wife, my kids, my family, and friends, and those who are seeking to find peace in a peaceful place.

In a world that is full of uncertainties we are searching and looking for things to lift our spirits. As well, we are looking to be loved and valued.

Your days may seem dark but there is a light inside you that will take you through the darkness. So, I give you a look into my soul, so you can look into yours, and find that light that shines in you that will lead you to your peaceful place.

Contents

Acknowledgments

Writing a book is harder than I thought but it is rewarding at the same time. The world can be a better place if each of us uses their gifts to develop and create leaders in the world. We must not be selfish but selfless with who we are. What will make this world a better place is if we share our gifts and time to mentor future leaders. My thanks to everyone who saw me grow and encouraged me to realize my potential.

To all the individuals that I have watched lead others, you have inspired me as well. My hope for everyone who reads this book is that they are inspired to find their own gift in themselves, embrace it and share it with others.

Without the support of my peers, this book would not exist. All of you have shown me what great leaders are made of. Thanks to each and every one of you for your inspiration. Having an idea and turning it into a book is as hard as it sounds. The experience was internally challenging as well, and I'm grateful to everyone who walked this journey with me.

To my kids: Mykaila, Kyai and Josiah, when I look at you guys, I see life and that's why I continue to do my best in my own life. I love you guys with my breath, my heart, my soul.

My Grandma, Lynet May Butler, who raised me from a little boy in Jamaica, instilled in me the character of the man I am today.

My Mama: this woman is like the air I breathe. Casita Butler, I love you forever. Your prayers gave me the strength that I need when I was lost and weak. You taught me discipline and told me never to give up on anything.

All my brothers and sisters: Paulette, Dean, Michael, Annette, Margaret and Carol. All of you have played a vital role in my life. Your encouragement and confidence in me gave me the will to continue to push forward in spite of adversity.

My nieces and nephews: Trisha, Tenisha, Travis, Akash, Sanjana. Each of you has played a vital role in my life and I thank you guys for who you are and what you have meant to me.

My wife, who has encouraged me from the beginning, I appreciate and love you so much. I pray that God continues to watch over us as we go through this journey called life.

My friends: Danny Stone, Lovemore Sher Mclaughlin, Nicole

Waldron, Dr. Vibe, Destiny Savary, Natalee Johnson, Petra James, Brother Gordon—my mentor and good friend—all of you are great examples of the ideal human being. I look up to each one of you and I thank you all for setting a good example for me to follow.

My editor and publisher: Cheryl Antao-Xavier. You have been a Godsend to me in many ways. Getting this book done has been challenging but you came along and made it easy for me, guiding me, explaining, and showing me the process. You were placed in my life for a reason, and I thank God for you.

I want to thank EVERYONE who ever said anything positive to me or taught me something. I heard it all, and it meant something, and it stayed with me.

I want to thank God most of all, because without God I wouldn't be able to do any of this.

Colin

Introduction

Why do certain poetry books or poems grab a hold of someone's imagination? Well, the pain of being in a dark place in your life will take you to places you never knew existed. Then you find your strength deep in your soul and your gift just starts to manifest in you.

Writing true poetry is not waking up in the morning and saying I'm going to be a poet; it comes from a place where God meets you and says, "I grant you this gift, this talent. Now use it for my glory to free yourself and the minds of my people."

Message from a Dear Supporter

Moments Before My Dad passed!

God places us at the right place at the right time!

Around 8am on Friday, January 29th, 2021, I received a call from the local hospital. The doctor informed me that my dad was not going to last the weekend.

I called the hospital Chaplain and asked him to meet me at my dad's bedside at 11am. He was on time, we sat on each side of the bed and throughout my cellphone played my dad's favourite hymns and intermittently prayed for him. I had never experienced death and really didn't know what to expect. All I knew was that my dad was religious, and I thought he would love us to pray with him.

About noon that day, a member of the hospital cleaning staff came to the door on hearing the hymns. My eyes connected with him as he turned away to leave the room and I beckoned him that it was okay for him to get his cleaning done. Being in the hospital during COVID I would want my dad's room cleaned as I always wanted the best for him. Moments later, this gentleman dropped the cleaning equipment and walked over to the foot of the bed and asked permission of the Chaplain and me to pray with us. I felt the strength of his prayer uplift both of us. It was as if he brought that final message that we all wanted to hear. I believe it also reached my dad; he was hearing us.

On Friday, after being at his bedside all day he left us within 30 minutes of me leaving the room. He was supported that final day by the hospital's Chaplain, the gentlest nurse I have ever experienced – she had been with him all week, and a member of the hospital's cleaning staff, Colin Jones, who also spent time praying with him. Colin had walked into the room and sat at the foot of my dad's bed and his prayer was so powerful–we were in awe when he finished. He also went back and prayed alone with my dad just after he passed.

Colin requested that I read a poem that he had recently written at my dad's funeral.

(NOTE: The poem is written in third and first person, so please listen for the transition. The poem is on the next page: 'Another Angel in the Sky')

Another Angel in the Sky

by Colin Jones

Another LIFE has gone, but heaven, here comes
another ANGEL unto you, with white angelic wings,
spreading far and wide,
What a BEAUTIFUL sight to see you were SET FREE,
ANGEL IN THE SKY your new life has just begun,
…It is your time to SHINE under God's marvelous LIGHT, ….
No more pain as you take FLIGHT
so you can look down on your family, day and night

———————————

Don't worry I see you—God has placed my spirit in ALL OF YOU
I heard the trumpet, and the voice of God called me,
I am with the Angels now, DANCING because
God has set me FREE,
no more pain, no more tears but pure joy and happiness
as I set my wings like an eagle and SOAR IN THE SKY
Pray to YOUR Father and he will open YOUR eyes
and give YOU sight to see me as I pass over YOU
with that marvelous shadow of LIGHT.
I am your Angelic Angel, my father called ME, and I had to go,
do not cry for ME,
CELEBRATE with me,
let my life on earth BE for something and not for nothing,
I feel your tears already even though you have not shed one drop,
save your tears, for another day will come
that is more important than MINE,
I am with MY Father NOW and ETERNAL LIFE IS MINE.
YOUR ANGELIC ANGEL IN THE SKY

The Soul of a Man

Why me, God?

You have called me into existence and in my dreams, You have shown me many things. You gave me sight to see things that human eyes cannot see, and you have put me in a position to succeed. In this position, I've already seen the amazing things you are doing through me. But God, tell me why have you chosen me?

This gift that I have is not for the weak. So, I hope and pray you continue to give me the strength to do Your Will.

My faith and hope are at an all-time high and when I walk into a room, I carry Your spirit and Your light with me. I smile all day, because I know where You have brought me from and where I'm going. I know You will always be with me. This vessel that I am walks in this world, but my spirit and soul reside with You. As I gaze outside my window, I feel Your presence around me. I am so grateful to know You and Your creation before me.

I also thank You for the breath of life. I have prayed for the gift of healing, but I finally realize it's already in me. I share this gift in what I write. I share my soul with all who will hear me.

Food for the Soul

If I give you a seat at my table with an empty plate before you, you will probably think that I am crazy for not giving you something to eat. But the food I'm about to give you will last you forever.

Close your eyes and listen to my soul speak because the food I give has deep impact. My soul is the Father/Son and the Holy Spirit in me. Now, do you see what I mean.

I feel the pain of the world with every beat of my heart and my soul cries every day. I search for things to say while I pray.

God has said: "Mankind must change their ways. There are those who do not believe and they teach false doctrine in My name. That's why My world is in pain. But do not worry about this, because My Son is coming back again."

This is the food for the soul that I had to give you, and if you read His Word it will continue to fill you and sustain your life.

Take My Hand ~ says the Lord

God says: "Take My hand, walk with Me and I will bring you peace. Open your ears and your heart, receive My words so it will never leave you.

Your soul will be a part of Me, and My Spirit will set you free. Look to the sky and on your knees pray to Me. Yet if your words are empty with no real substance, it won't reach Me.

The air you breathe, I've given it to you for free. The time you live is not set in stone until I call you home. My door will always be open. But my Son has to be pleased with you. So choose the right path, repent of your sins, and come to me in baptism."

He is my Rock

His rock is my salvation on which I stand. I stand by His word because that is my foundation. I will continue to build on this rock, this foundation, by being true to His word.

Take me, Lord, to the place You have in store for me.
I want to bask in Your glory.
I know You are building a house around me
and that's of the beautiful people that surround me.
I've seen my place in Your kingdom. I've seen it in my dreams.
I thank you Lord for preparing me to do
whatever I need to do to carry out Your will.
I stand by Your every word. I hear your voice in the wind,
urging me to move for You have more for me to do.
Take me wherever You may but if You stand by me,
I will always be free.
Without You there is no life in me.
God, You are the center, the core of me.

He Resides in the Soul

I wrap my arms around myself to embrace Him because the life that is in me is of Him.

There is more than one place to find Him. He is everywhere.

He chose me to be who I am and the words I speak is not from an ordinary man.

Open your eyes and look deep into my eyes and you will see Him looking back at you.

He resides in my soul that He created in me.

The Lord has given me permission to write the words I write and speak the words I speak—that's His blessings on me.

It has been a long soul journey to this present state. He found me in the darkest of places where life had abandoned me. He brought me out of there.

I promised Him obedience. Opened my arms and my heart to Him.

There is no place I would not go to find Him. He resides in the soul—in my soul.

The right time is anytime to find Him, just open your hearts and let Him in.

Towards a Full Heart

There was a time when my heart left me. I felt like I had no life. I was breathing but I felt empty. I was alone with no one around me.

Loneliness gripped me even when I lived in a house that was full yet felt empty. My strength was taken away from me.

I cried out: Lord, take me because I have lost everyone and everything.

Little did I know He was testing me. I was down on my knees in humility and defeat when God heard me.

"Son," He said to me, "you have more strength than you know. Just take my hand and walk with me for I will give you life and everything you need. Never look back because where I'm taking you is holy ground. Your feet will not fail you if you walk in My footsteps.

"It will not be easy because where you are going, only I can lead you. Let no one deceive you. Listen for My voice and only move as I tell you. Now go for I have given you something that no one can take away from you. A soul that has life and a heart that is full of love and compassion. You will never be lonely. You will never be empty."

Love my Soul

If my tears could give you life, I would cry until the end of time. If my smile could brighten your day, well here you go, I will smile all day. Let my words make your heart dance.

Let my soul be the thing you love about me because it holds everything in me.

Will you pray for me not because I pray for you but because I need prayers to.

We stand together as one even though we are many.

The Wword of the Lord will give us strength such that no enemy will prevail. His words are our force field.

When your soul meets the Father, the excitement is such that cannot be explained. I tell you your blessings will rain on you each and every day. Let His grace sustain you and his love fill your being.

Don't you worry for the eyes of the Lord will always be on you.

There is so much more to say but I will leave it for another day. The Lord has blessed me with these words just for today.

Know the Enemy

The Lord said:
"Your soul was wounded, and I healed you.
Stay faithful to this path because I need you.
Your obedience is evident in everything you do.
Every step you take along the way
There will surely be a test for you.
Never be complicit and know who's around you.
The enemy will surround you
With people who pretend to love you.
I've given you a soul that will
Unveil the foxes around you."

My Soul sees Evil

You may silence me with your hate, but my soul sees through to your evil ways. I see your true nature when I look into your eyes. My soul has stripped away your false disguise. You may look like a sheep, but you are a fox in sheep's clothing. I see through to you.

If you come to me with truth and advice, make sure there are no lies couched in your words.

I see the darkness in you and I'm trying to show you the way back to the truth, but the hate that's inside of you is holding you fast.

I've gone through too much and my soul is now able to see the evil in others. I've been given this gift to recognize evil when I see it and I will use this talent to expose you. I will use my words to rebuke you. A rebuke is not to hurt you it's to drive the evil out of you.

Take a journey with me and you will see what I see. The God that's in me, He will set you free.

Mould Me to Your Will, Lord

Purify my soul, Lord, and let my heart not be like hardened clay. Mould me, Lord, right here, right now, today.

The feeling inside me is so great that my heart is bursting with anticipation of what I can do with Your guidance.

I think of my grandmother, and I can hear her voice say, "Son, don't worry, because the light you follow will bring you to a brighter place."

I feel the strength of The One who lives within me even as I feel the hurt still there inside of me. I guess pain comes with life's purpose and I should not worry about it. My soul cannot hide my true feelings, but I trust the Lord with everything.

We search for things in the wrong places, and we don't look deep within for our healing, for our guidance.

God says "I'm with you and in you. I'm the only one who can heal you. The vessel that carries you gets stronger each day. Don't worry, I will never let your heart become like hardened clay for I will pour life into it each day. Never let what I give you go to waste."

Arising Spirit

I arise this morning with my heart in my soul and my soul in my spirit.

I give God thanks for everything in me because without him I am empty. He feeds me and I am filled. He holds me to protect me, and my path is guided by Him.

True love is constant, and I know His love is over me. I know His mercy for I have seen it in my life. His grace is always with me. He is always with me.

He fills my words with substance. He moulds me and rebuilds me every day that I breathe.

He believes in me. 'Follow my lead,' He tells me. 'And the light of my Son will guide you to eternity. Nothing will harm you because I will always be with you.'

I hear the voice of the Lord when I close my eyes to pray. This is what He said to me: "Thank you son for acknowledging Me today and every other day you kneel to pray. Your words mean a lot to me because you show true faith in me. Many times, I've put you to the test, but you stayed obedient and didn't walk away from Me."

I will kneel on the ground and praise You every day, Lord God. I cleanse myself with Your words, Lord. Society can't judge me. I look to You Father because You are The One who created me.

The closer I get to You, Father, the more I have a clear vision of You. My eyes have never seen anything that's more divine. Thank you for Your guiding light for even when night falls, I can still see You.

Inspiration in a Seashell

A seashell in the sand—God's creation in my hands. As I put it to my ears, I hear the sound of life and of peace. The sounds carry cries to heal the land, speaking to me as I continue on my life's journey.

As I look across this stretch of white sand, all I can see is the great blue sea. Lord, help me to get to the other side—the true purpose of my life—because that's where I know You are leading me. There is something special on the other side waiting for me. I know it with a certainty I feel deep in my soul.

I made my bed in the sand by the sea and woke up to find a path created for me. I ran as fast as I could towards this beautiful light in front of me, only to realize it was leading me towards my destiny.

In my soul I carry the plan You have for me. In my heart I carry the love You have shown me.

Lord, I thank you for the sounds, the inspiration that You gave me through this seashell I hold in my hands.

My Life is Your Life, Lord

In resurrection we rise again but what we do with that new life is another thing. I rise in resurrection to live for Christ. I see it as my new life, and this is what I intend to do with it.

To be baptized in the living water and be part of Christ is an amazing thing. It puts you in connection with the Father because the only way to the Creator is through the Son. Who do you want in your corner when it seems the world is against you, and you go through difficult times.

I chose the Son of man because He shed His blood for my sins. I will fight by His side until the end because I know my end will be the beginning of great things. When I open my eyes, He opens His with me. When I breathe, He breathes with me. I walk in righteousness, but I know it's not easy. My life is not perfect, but I know He does not look for perfection in me. I show Him my vulnerability because nothing can ever be hidden from Him. The deeper I go into my soul I enter another realm. The spirit is not hard to understand but you must be connected to the Spirit. His words nourish my soul and energize my blood, giving me oxygen to breathe and to be purified.

The deeper you are connected to Him you will understand the life that's within you. My life is your life, God. You are everything to me. My eyes can only see the goodness and blessings before me. His grace and salvation cover me.

He Tests Us

My soul has left my body and I feel empty.
I search for love and humanity but can't find it in me.
I struggle day in and day out
I ask myself why this has happened to me.
People with their cruel ways creep up behind me
and I have no strength to keep them away.
Temptation surrounds me, and my mind gets foggy.
What scared me most
was that I felt my foundation give way beneath me.
I felt I was sinking each day.
I wandered into the darkness and the most beautiful thing happened
My legs got weak, and I was brought to my knees.
I began to weep. Through my tears, I heard this voice.
It boomed like thunder, and it scared me.
The voice said to me, "I was testing you
to see who you seek in time of need.
I am the Father who created you,
The One who took your soul away.
But you kept your faith and didn't denounce me.
I have released your soul back to you.
The strength you have now is like no other
and an abundance of blessings will follow you.
All this, because you were faithful to me.
Your obedience has set your soul free."

When Two Souls Meet

We crossed paths and you were so kind to me. Your smile drew me, and your soul spoke to me.

It happened because God wanted us to meet. You may have thought it was business, but it was more than that to me. Sometimes when you meet a person, they make the light shine brighter in your life.

We met more than once but it felt like a thousand times to me. Your kindness was special, and it meant a lot to me.

I will never forget you and I hope you are looking down on me.

God had a plan for you that's why you were called to heaven. Your kids miss you and I know you love them too.

You lived your life to the fullest, but I wish you had more time to enjoy it. Heaven called you, my friend, and here on Earth, we thank you for blessing us with your presence.

Finding You, Lord

If I would have known You wouldn't be here when I was born, I would've given my life to be with You. I heard about You from the mouths of others and my heart was filled with joy and anticipation of knowing You. They spoke about You so eloquently and said You were brilliant beyond their wildest dreams, with Your eyes so bright. Not one word was spoken but in silence they heard You speak.

His heart was pure, and His love was unwavering. The kindness He showed was next to nothing, a man with no sin but they still judged Him. Their eyes could not believe what they saw and felt when healing coursed through their bodies.

Multitudes followed Him and there were many who wanted to prosecute Him. To fear death is one thing but to be hated by the ones who say they love you is another thing. They pierced Your heart with words of hate, chained You, locked You up for no reason, whipped You. Yet You still loved them.

What kind of love is this, I need to know it. From my soul I will tell Your story and my spirit will show Your glory, my emotions will channel Your story. Your name I will proclaim.

Your truth lies within me and there I will hold it so I can praise Your name.

My Leading Light

Can I lead you out of the darkness with the light that is in me? I am here to tell you the truth because that's what's in me. I'm led by The One who created me and that's what I'm trying to share with you because of what He has done for me. There were days that were dark, and I had a heart full of pain. With so much hurt, my mind was clouded by the confusion of this world, and I tried to close my eyes to the things I see but, in my dreams, everything just came back to me.

I lead with love and along the way throughout my journey I gained wisdom and knowledge. Forgiveness was a hard part of my journey because I could not forgive those who hurt me. Grace has mended my heart and I have learned to forgive from the lessons He has taught me and now the life that I live my God has made amazing for me.

I am open to hear you speak but I will discern the truth in it. We are in a time where anyone can preach and quote Scriptures to you and me.

The music the angels play sets me up for a bright and successful day, so I open my ears to hear the orchestra play and the voice of the conductor (God) on this day.

He Chose Me

I was chosen when I was broken, at my lowest point, because God knew I needed Him. This life that I live, I cannot live without Him. Teach me, Lord, for Your way is the only way and Your walk is the only walk. The chains are broken, and my eyes are open, but Lord, there is still something I'm not seeing.

Here I am on my knees with my face to the ground, crying out to you, Lord. I need to know You more. I have cried so many nights from what I feel inside. This world that I live in has so much hate in it and I'm burdened by it.

People have fallen or walked away from You. They try to change our perceptions of how we see and view You. We fight, but they crucify us with man-made laws. People become like slithering snakes, crawling in the grass, fallowing the fallen one's ways.

Anything gained from evil jealousy and backbiting will be the bed of our sorrows and pain until Judgement Day.

Hold on to what God has given you and look to man for nothing.

Fast and pray for all your needs and wait on heaven for your true blessings.

No man can take away the blessings that God bestowed on you.

Heal Me Lord

The Lord helps me to be humble and not lash out at the things I see and feel in this world. Sometimes I'm tired and I shed tears when I can't take it anymore. Even though I feel broken at times I still invite people inside.

My soul is full of an abundance of love and kindness but sometimes I want to just cover up and hide it. When it's burdened and hurt, the soul of a man will go into hiding. Yet the goodness of a man should never be hidden. I judge no one.

I tell you where my feelings are coming from, but people will see what they want to see, and they don't see this beautiful soul inside of me. Why does love hurt so much? My heart swells, I feel the pounding in my chest, and I ask God to heal the rest but as day breaks and I feel the sun shining down on me I know it's God watching over me.

My precious heart, the engine of my soul and my spirit, you never lie to me, you always reveal everything in time so my eyes can see. Touch me Lord and heal everything inside of me, strengthen me Lord so when the pain comes, I know it's you that I need, if I say I wish I never loved like this, the world will miss the greatness and passion that God has placed inside of me, true love conquers all and that's what I have inside of me.

Soul Testimony

I have given you my testimony, now tell me what you will do with it. I embrace you and hope you will stand by me. You say you are a man of God and a mentor. I hope it's true and not a lie.

I spoke to her, and she quoted Scriptures so eloquently that I believed her. But something happened that made me think twice about her.

I entrusted others with my testimony, but God showed me something in a dream that I couldn't believe! "Do not judge them if they have become silent to you," God said. "You are on a path to purpose. No matter what they say or do, I have given you the will to overcome difficulties and that's one of your strengths."

I was broken because of the silence, but maybe it's a good thing I distanced myself from that energy. Refocus is what I need to do, and I will look to the stars to find You, and if my vision fails me in my dream, I will see You.

My testimony is with Him and that's the only thing that should matter to me.

Help me, oh God, to forgive those who have wronged me and the ones who do not believe in me. You have put your stamp on my life, and I continue to see Your guiding light. I will wait before I proceed because only You can lead me.

Let Your words be the food that sustains me and Your unfailing love be the protection that I need.

A Beautiful Light

What a wonderful feeling it is when your light shines from within and you feel something special is coming through you. You see the transformation happen as your revival makes your purpose become clear.

So, I compose myself and wonder what is truly happening. How am I being received. They take my love and kindness for granted and expect me to do nothing. I've been hurt and verbally abused with words of hate murmured in silence, so you don't hear my voice.

I hear my Father calling me, and He says: "Place yourself before my altar and I will take away your pain. People may doubt you for what you do and say but continue to do what I ask of you. I have placed something great inside your soul, yet make no mistake, the enemy will come after you. Fear not because your Angel is watching over you. I see and hear the words you write and speak. I know they have made a difference in someone's life.

You walk with the spirit of three, the Father, the Son and the Holy Spirit."

Precious Life

Life is a precious thing. We rise with the sun. We lie in our bed not knowing what the day will bring. But when our eyes open to live another day, we must praise Him.

When my eyes open, the tears flow and with every teardrop I thank God for life. His name is the first word that comes from my mouth in praise. And as night falls, He is the door keeper of my soul, spirit, mind, and heart.

He listens and acts in His own time that's why I'm patient with Him. His house is my house and that's where I worship him. In alone time in silence, I withdraw to my closet in the darkness and summon my God with yearning from within, weeping and crying. When things go wrong and there is no sign of Him, I wonder if He is watching or even listening.

"Why do you question me," is what I hear in the stillness as He speaks to me.

My God forgive me it's only because I feel the enemy is after me.

"I have put you in a position to succeed and no matter what the enemy tries they do not supersede My wishes. I am heaven and earth and I hold the key to coming and going, no one does anything without Me seeing and knowing. Your life is my life, and no one can change anything unless I allow it. I am God who created everything."

Road to My Purpose

I am determined to persevere into the future. I know it is a long road with many roadblocks ahead of me. I know a Man who went ahead to pave the way for us. The turbulence in my mind blinded me from seeing things. So, I went to The One who created me. This is what He said: "Free your mind from confusion, mistrust and worry. Learn to trust and forgive."

His voice was like thunder. I understand the trust He has in me. His gift came as a supernatural feeling over me. It opened my eyes, and I began to see meaning in my life. My mind is a precious thing, it orchestrates everything from within.

This journey is amazing and with every step I can feel His presence.

Meekness in Me

Let me humble myself so I can come to You in meekness. Will You nurture my soul so my entire being can be as one. If I am troubled, I will seek You and find You and meekly ask Your permission to approach You. I am willing to be submissive to Your will. I promise obedience wherever I stand. Draw me near because I want to be close to You. Let my virtue be the meekness that You seek for in me. My love and kindness are real.

I feast on what is real and hunger for more of what is right. You keep me calm, so I do not rise up like a storm in the night. I give You all authority over me, my God, to keep my strength intact, because with You I can never lose. Choosing to be this person is not an option because I know who You are; You are the Father of Creation that's brought me this far.

Let humility clothe me and the righteousness of my soul be all of me. Let my beginnings never end and when my end comes let it be my beginning.

He Called Me

Though I'm alive and I feel blessed, my spirit is calling out to me that it's not time to rest yet. And I know my work has only just begun. God says "greater things are coming, and I will give you strength to meet these challenges. I have shown you love through the wife and child that I have placed by your side. Mountains will stand in your way, but I will move them for you. Your eyes will see things but only because I let you."

God tells me, "People will revolt against you because of what I have placed in you—the spirit of a Phoenix and the light of Christ that is in you."

I will not rest until I carry out Your request. I will not fold, nor will I be moved. I am guarded by the Angels who watch over me. Lord, I know there is more for me to do but prepare me through and through. Your people do not see me even in the house where I worship You. Thank you for Your glory and I will continue to pave a way and let my life according to You tell a story.

Nothing will stop me because many more doors will be opened for me. I cannot wait to see the next chapter of my life with my wife and child by my side. Many stories will be told but I put You, God, first in my life.

Phoenix Spirit

I had a dream one night where I was a Phoenix taking flight. A bird so angelic yet powerful, I thought: "my God, what is this tonight?"

My dream showed me that I was evolving into something great. God, I ask of you to prepare me for what's coming. I feel it in the blood coursing through my veins. It's like I'm becoming stronger each day in my own way.

This is a different kind of strength, and I am shown how to use it, so I don't abuse it. My heart is full, my soul is overflowing. Tell me God what will my spirit do? I feel so enlightened and am trying to understand what's becoming of me. I know the enemy will come after me but You, God, will stand with me.

"My son," He says to me in my dream, "I'm giving you the spirit of a Phoenix. Don't take it lightly. The spirit of Me is also with you, now arise and open your eyes, it's a brand-new day for I have given you life to see another day."

Share the Peace and Joy

Woke up this morning with great peace and joy in my heart.
And the joy spilled into a smile on my face.
I wanted to share this great peace with everyone.
I share the peace that's within me.
God's joy is my joy. He fills my life with peace and joy.
I smile because I know what I've been through
He brought me through those dark days.
Are you willing to hear what I have to say?
I can tell you how to find your way.
It's a lesson you can take and be on your way.
Please do not judge me when I give you my life history
I am showing you how God found me.
Hold on to your faith
Follow the light
There is nowhere for you to hide
Because God will always find you.

Passing on His Words

He says to me: "I created you not to be ordinary, but extraordinary,
But don't think you are better than anyone.
Pass on My words through the gift I have given you.
Write my words in poetry.
The strength you possess through writing will reach others."
I close my eyes to look deep within myself
To find perseverance and the will to survive.
But I still do not understand why You have chosen me, God.
Your world is heavy on my heart
And the tears of Your people draw me to them.
I open my heart, my spirit and my soul to You.
I know I'm not better than anyone.
But I thank You God for making me extraordinary.

Freedom from Depression

Those of you who suffer depression know that it will control you. It will hold you in silence until you are powerless.

You are confused in a world that abuses God's Word and the teachings of Christ. It tells you this is how you should live and what you should do.

These false words control your mind and hold you in this imaginary place that does not exist in reality. It confuses your mind until you go blind to the true meaning of life and what it truly means to exist.

Depression runs deep and it controls the rhythm of the heartbeat. It stirs up trouble on the inside. Decision-making becomes lost in the fog of your mind. Your personality is compromised, as depression takes hold and loneliness becomes part of your life.

I tell you this: Hold yourself in stillness and let your soul speak and watch the closed door of depression open to set you free. Don't be sad, be glad as history will not repeat itself if you have opened your soul to let Christ in. Depression will leave your mind.

Gather yourself and embrace the gift that's inside of you. Remember, whatever you have been through, God's got you. Your freedom from depression will shine through in your smile.

Die in Yourself to Awaken Your Soul

My eyes have seen true living. If you walk with Christ, you will have eternal life. It is with the Father's permission that I see this. How can I explain this truth to you if you don't believe in His teaching. He shed His blood on the cross, died on the cross. We must remember this lesson.

You have to die in your ego self to become one of the livings who walk with Him. Take a moment to be silent and to understand what I'm saying.

The teacher teaches and students listen in obedience. Most importantly, your soul must be ready to receive His teachings because every parable will open your soul to the truth.

There is a path to Him, but it is not an easy one. He will take you through troubled waters—you must just have faith and believe in Him.

Keep the cross close to your heart because freedom comes with it. His name is Jesus and He will lead the way to Truth and eternity.

Eyes of God Upon Us

Only He can see me when nobody else can. All my life I've been giving and lending a hand to others. I pour out my heart and soul, but no one really opens their eyes to truly see me. They are blind to my existence but not to my giving.

My spirit is hurting, and my insides are crying, but I thank God for my blessings because only He can see me. I wonder sometimes what is in the minds of others when they encounter love and humanity. What do they do when kindness is shown to them. Can you see me because I can see you, I give you what He gives me and that's the beauty of what lies within my soul.

I rise when they put me down because of who stands beside me. The true king wears His crown, but I place His cross in my heart. When I come to you with joy and humility, I come with The One who created you and me. I place God above all things and am humble before Him.

Look into my eyes and you will see life and that's because of who created me. If you still choose not to see me that's okay because God's eyes are always on me. For the rest of my life, I choose light over everything so that in darkness I can see. Through my eyes I will turn your darkness into life, the spirit of The One who created me is looking right back at you.

Now do you see me?

Calling My Name

After calling out His name my life changed. That's the moment He spoke to me. My eyes opened to see so many things. He delivered me from my sins and the dark place that I was in.

He revived me and filled my soul with grace. In my mind I played it back many times on my journey, trying to understand why I went through those difficult times. The pain was so excruciating, but I still had faith in Him.

Can you hear Him (God)? I can because I have given Him my life and opened everything to Him. Teach me and I will follow, I said. With wisdom I will grow, guide me and I will find You.

My path goes through the one who is like You (Jesus). I will shout from the highest place so the world can hear Your name. You walked the walk and you talked to talk even in Your last few days on earth. Your light will always shine on me because You (God) has a purpose for me. I will do Your will no matter what is placed in front of me. Even with my last breath I will praise Your name, Jesus.

Footprints in the Sand

Jesus walked for miles and walked on water for you and me. He gave His life on the cross and died for our sins. Who am I? I am Him with arms wide open. He called me and accepted me in. I am Him who walked in the rain and received God's showers of blessings from heaven. I am the one who walks with the light of Him in my soul. I am the one who cannot move without taking God with me. A place of love and humanity He has placed in me.

A soul so bright like the stars in the sky, it's the only place I want to be. I find my peace as I place my feet in His footprints in the sand. A journey so challenging, in my mind I may have struggled sometimes but my struggles lead to my greatest strength—my faith.

Jesus, I have no shame. I call out Your name Jesus. It's imprinted in my heart and will always be that way.

Soul Cry

Bruised and broken, pain on the inside, tears like rain falling. I feel like chains are holding me back. I wonder in my mind if I'm lost. But I'm not. One day they love you and the next they don't. I share my aspirations with you, and I trust you with my soul. But you tear me down behind my back like a wolf devouring his prey.

I saw you from afar and God said to help you find your way. I said, "Lord, why me for this is the one who has hurt me? I know I must forgive because You died for us and took away our sins."

My soul is peace, and you can hear it, feel it, when I speak. My spirit is like the sea, like restless raging water I'm ready to cover all. But I act with the Lord. I pray my soul will accept you but let me remind you I walk with the One who created you.

For You My Friend

You were called into existence for a reason and a purpose. He placed you in a position of authority to make a difference and gave you words to uplift His people.

Your soul is a most beautiful place, and, in your presence, I can see it shining in your eyes. Your words are so inspiring, you tell no lies but give life. The spirit in you lights up the darkness that clouds your world and that's because of Who lives in you.

You are blessed not to impress but to give life to those who do not believe. You walk with confidence because His blessings are all over you. The most important thing is His Angels are watching over you.

Selfless is how I see you as you give to those who don't even know you. God knows your heart and that's is good.

An angel is who you are—a most beautiful star.

Telling My Ancestors' Story

As I closed my eyes my mind took me back in time. Drums were beating and many were dancing. What a lively sight to see!

I laid my head down to rest and was gripped in a terrible dream. The pain was so real, it brought me to my knees. I can see them leading you away like stray dogs. You tried to run but they took your legs, you raised your hands and those were gone as well. They broke your will with the evil things they did.

Life as you knew it was at a standstill. There were chains and whips and guns to your head. You were dragged onto that dreadful ship. I heard your cry echo in the sound of the slave master's whip. Adrenaline pumping, not knowing how to save yourselves. Eyes wide open in terror.

A boom sounded in my ears as black smoke filled the air. In my dream I watched you fall to the ground with no sound. Not an ounce of blood was lost because it went back into the dust from where you were created. Crucified like Christ, but there was no cross. They laid you side by side and that's how you died. Some splayed out in the shape of a cross. Some bodies cast overboard into the deep sea. You did not know then that death was better than slavery.

For what kind of human is this with skin white as the clouds and eyes blue as the sea, yet with no love in their hearts. Filled with hate and evil deep within their souls. They claim to come in peace but evil they brought to a land rich with plenty, enough for all, where my ancestors stood proud. Africa my home, a land rich and plenty like heaven, flowing with milk and honey.

My eyes have seen the glory as I continue to tell my ancestors' story. We will rise again as we continue to beat the drums of our African ancestors' endurance and power.

Summon Your Prayer Warrior

The people of the world are in trouble and crying out for help. Too many people are dying at the hand of their enemies. Greed and jealousy are dividing the church.

The word of God is not a lie. It's time to summon the prayer warrior within us. I have opened the door for you to start something big. You must know this about me, if you are close to me, I can see what you see and feel what you feel. But know that it's not me but God that is in me who sees this. My body is like an antenna that receives the signals God sends to me. My soul is the gateway to Him as Christ who lives in me is the only way to Him.

I write this with a great sense of urgency because I feel something is coming that's greater than you and me. I cannot explain it but my body shivers when I think about it. God told me to tell you there is a shift coming so get yourself ready and prepare for it. There is a burning sensation in my spirit, and I feel that what I write can give you life, but you must believe in it. He is the conductor of my vessel that holds everything in me. I trust Him. God has put something special in me.

Remember Him in Troubled Times

In troubled times, turn to The One who created you. When people fail you, He will always be with you to see you through. I give you strength to fight.

He says, "There is life in you for I, the One who created heaven and Earth lives in you. Darkness may consume you, but the light of my Son will find you and guide you."

Don't be afraid to cry because God hears tears. Take all your troubles to Him and He will turn it around and grant your blessing. Close your eyes and visualize the Creator in you—then you will understand that faith and hope live in you.

Stand tall and never bow down to the hate and the evil ways of society. That's what the enemy wants you to do. Instead open your soul and look deep inside to your truth and you will see the greatness in you.

Carry all your burdens to Him. Never forget He will never fail you.

Deep Love--Peace

His love is deeper than the deepest waters to me. Open your eyes, I say, and look upon His signs and wonders. His love is precious. His forgiveness is forever. Embrace the life that He has chosen for you because He has never failed you.

Spirit of the living Father, I hear your voice and I will never ignore you. My calling is in Your every word and Your spirit will bring me through. I can see the things You see and speak the language of the Holy Spirit. Teach me Lord to speak to You in this language of tongues that You have given me. It's truly awesome what You have put in me. The peace that I feel is amazing. That's why I can worship You with peace in my soul.

Replacing My Pain Shadow With His Grace

I sometimes smile to hide my pain and hope for healing rains to wash away my pain. The Lord is the keeper of my tears for when I cry you cannot see my tears. They flow on the inside.

It hurts so much when you think you have done right, but it ends up being wrong. All you can do is pray to God so He can turn it around for you.

As you go through your pain, you learn that childhood trauma and adult pain may be in different situations but the pain rages through you just the same.

Sometimes in my dreams I see my pain shadow following me. I can only run from it for so long and hide from it, but the pain shadow finds me. I believe in The One who created me and now it's time to find Him so He can heal me again.

The journey to Him was not easy and there were many times I did not believe in myself. But the deeper I went and searched within my soul, I started to believe in myself.

I found Him when I was on my knees and I said to him: "Please Lord, I cannot cry anymore. The pain is too deep, it has touched my soul. My spirit reaches out for You. Hold my hands, Lord, and give me the strength to continue to follow you."

With those words, He lifted me up and since then He has always been by my side.

My Soul—Where Peace Resides

My soul is the place where I find my peace. My cup overflows when the Holy Spirit speaks to me.

"Arise," He says, "and meet Me where you find your peace. I am everywhere. Even before you were born, I knew you. The place where you found Me is where I always want to meet you. Your soul will overflow with love and what I give you. But nothing will enter your soul if it is corrupted with the sins of this world."

And I replied: I will consecrate my soul to You and give You access, Lord. I cannot walk away from You. My mind is Yours. So teach me, Father, because I need to know more about You. It is time because I know now that I am of You.

Tears of Pain

I wonder why I feel so much pain and yet it's not a physical pain. God, can you tell me why I'm crying. The feeling of burden is heavy on my mind and this burden is not even mine. Tell me who I'm becoming and why did You choose me to be this way.

I feel sorrow for Your people and a lot of them are in pain. They have walked away from Your path and the evil of society has captured their mind. Their eyes have turned away from You and their souls are no longer open to the things that are of You. They hide their pain, and their eyes are dry like the arid desert.

Who am I that I feel the pain of Your people with my eyes flowing with tears like the River Jordan.

I know why tears fall from my eyes and why I feel pain. Give me, Lord, what You need to give them, and I will teach them and show them that there's no other way but the right way through the blood of Your Son.

If I must cry and feel pain until they find their way to You, then let it be so. I'm on my way.

No Easy Path

I know nothing will come easy to me on this path, Lord. And I'm humbled because Your light will always guide me. My soul is on the path of righteousness.

The spirit of the Lord tells me the Father is pleased with me. Let His grace cover me wherever I may lay, for when night falls it is You that protects me in my sleep.

The feeling I get when the Lord speaks to me is something I cannot explain but it's beautiful. When the tears start to run down my face, it comes from a place deep within me. Catch my tears, Lord, for I weep for Your world.

Vine of Life

My soul tells me the vine of life runs through me. I ask myself what this means to me. The Lord has granted me life and His lifeblood circulates through my veins like a vine of life. I can tell you how it feels to me, it's wonderful and beautiful to me.

Thus, I am descended from a lineage of kings. The greatest of fathers, the one of many is a part of me. The strength of many protects me, that is why I'm never weak. I summon their wisdom from a place deep within me; a place beyond my soul; a deep realm of divinity.

Step inside this place, though I must tell you my soul is Holy ground because of The One who dwells there and steers me. That's why I could never be lost. I have been found and my ground is His ground where He walks. You won't hear me coming but the silence of my presence will be overwhelming. Don't be alarmed because I am peace and I bring peace with me.

Come close to me and feel my peace. It is in the soul in me.

I Feel His Crown

Would you wear His crown willingly if it was given to you? His pain was excruciating, but He bore it for you and me. They hammered a crown of thorns onto His head, and He cried out in pain. Would you have taken His place, or would you have denied Him like Peter did?

I hear His voice clearly in my sleep as the light shines brightly over me in my dream. I asked: "God, who could this be, calling out? Is it Your Son who died on the cross and rose from death on the third day? Who died for us all?"

I feel every drop of His blood that seeped from under the crown on His head flowed through to us, to me, to wipe away our sins. His pain I felt in my dreams, and it brought me to my knees. My God how could man be so cruel to any human, even though they did not know He came so that we may have life.

Every breath that I take gives me life. So, if I'm to wear His crown of thorns then so let it be. No pain can stop me because I know You suffered for me. So here I am, Lord, please use me as You will.

A Troubled Heart

My heart is in pieces because people take my love and kindness for weakness and shred me to bits. This hurt touches the deepest part of my soul and my anger and loneliness rise to overwhelm me. But as this hurt enters my soul where my peace resides, a beautiful calmness comes over me.

My spirit lights up and a voice says to me, "My son, talk to me." I need to be still, so I can speak to Him. My soul is troubled, and my spirit is restless with anger and thoughts of revenge.

So, I call out: "God, can you please help me and strengthen the spirit of forgiveness in me. Those who are trampling on my love and kindness are truly hurting me. Lord help me to understand why it hurts so much. Take away this pain."

As I gather up paper and pen, I write what's within but if you get closer to me you will understand what I mean about pain and suffering. And peace.

Night falls and my soul comes awake trying to understand what took place. As I close my eyes, I am reminded that my Father is within my peaceful place. He lives within my soul.

Help Me See, Lord

Sometimes I can't breathe. I feel as though life is squeezing the breath out me. Wherever I go someone is trying to take something out of me. This life is not easy. Breathe life into me, oh God. Please help me see me.

I cannot see myself because I'm seeing and thinking about everybody else. Can you see the true love coming from me to you to save you. I can give what God gave me, but will your soul be true to me.

Lord, will You guide me along this path? Will You walk beside me? Teach me, Lord, along the way because there is so much more to learn about You. Even though I lead others, a leader can also learn from You. Where is this journey taking me, God, only You know.

There's a picture in my mind, and it travels from my heart to my soul. The life of all runs through my veins. It is a caring and loving spirit that travels through me. This is what my enemies are trying to break.

Let Your ways be my ways so they can see You in me, God.

Father, I am troubled, but I won't let trouble distract me away from the path You want me to take. Those who mean no good to me, burden me with the cares of this world.

My heart consoles them so they can see the true meaning of me. A soul that is not perfect, but true to the meaning of life and Christ. Here I am. I stand as a man in Christ.

Soul Words from The Source

I cannot compose or contain myself. I need to share with you what God has placed in me. These words of empathy, encouragement, and love are what He has placed in me.

My soul is the place where my Father lives and never sleeps. It's where you will find the source of all these words coming from me. He is the driver of my soul and my spirit. I'm just the vessel that holds His spirit.

Every step you take as you enter my soul is holy. You will learn about me and know that this journey was never easy. Bruised and broken to the point where my life meant nothing, that's how and where He found me. Like a Diamond from the dirt, He picked me up, built me up and to this day, He continues to mould me.

So now here I am. I open my soul to you. But I ask that you be true to me because the Lord is The One who guides me.

Let Your Words Guide Them to Me

Let me pass through the seas so I can find you, Lord. I may not be able to walk on water but even if I go under, I know you will find me. In my dreams I feel like I'm swimming through deep waters with no end in sight to get to You.

Surrounded by sharks with eyes so dark I see it's the pain they hold. But I hear the Lord say, "take them to a higher place because that's where you will find Me."

He speaks to me in parables and it's so amazing that in my dreams He makes everything clear to me.

Here is my heart, soul, and spirit, Lord. Fill them up and let me know what to do. I'm living this life just for You and with Your words that You have placed in me, Your people will see the true meaning of You. Your grace has sustained me and no matter what happens in my life You will always be there for me.

Find Your Own Soul

There is something inside of me that is divine. The Word of God is there to guide us, but it's up to you and me to find Him inside our souls.

This world is so messed up and there are people who say they love you, but they turn a blind eye to your pain. When your back is turned, they burn you.

In times like these, ask God for help to show them the love that's inside your soul. For the light that burns bright in your soul is a constant reminder of what's inside of you and me.

Why I am this Way

I live for His people before I turn to myself. I choose to be this way because of my humanity. Living your humanity is not a selfish way.

Grant me favour, dear Father and protect my heart because the more I show love and kindness to people, they still try to tear me apart with their evil ways.

I question myself sometimes because the pain they inflict digs so deep. Am I built for this, Lord, because it hurts so much when I've tried to be true to You, despite their rejection.

I love the way You are leading me, Lord, and I will continue like this to the end of my days. But Father, grant me protection and cover me with your unfailing love.

When people ask why you are this way when they use and abuse you, I answer, I am who my Father says I am because He created me to be this way. I follow His lead so that I may never go astray but if I do, He will always lead me back to the right way.

I Must Go. My Father Needs Me

I'm returning to my Father.
Don't cry for me, celebrate me for now I'm free.
I have lived my life the way He wanted me to.
I have served Him night and day on my knees in prayer.
I fed a multitude with the words He gave me
Now He has a new assignment for me.
My wings, they are so awesome!
I can soar above the clouds in the sky like an eagle.
I can look down on you, and come to you when you need me.
Just call me and I will hear you
And send you strength through my words.
I can feel your tears and hear your voice.
I will carry it all with me, but we will talk another time.
The gate is open and the Father is calling me.
The Father needs me.

Impact Statements

Colin is a deep, thoughtful and eloquent writer. His poetry is captivating. It is thought-provoking and forces you to really analyze yourself. His works bring warmth and a surety that you are seen and heard. My prayer is that God continues to enrich and strengthen his skills that he can touch more lives with his beautiful artistry. ~ *Shaunda Renee*

Colin is definitely an angel sent from God. His poems are intriguing. He expresses his love for the Lord, his feelings for people, and his views on society on a whole. In this, he reminds me of David in the Bible. I know his poems will be an encouragement to his readers…this modern David. ~ *Gordon Robinson*

Your words speak to how God shows up in me. I am still in awe of how you understood me so well from a virtual lens. I love your passion of wanting to inspire, uplift and help to positively impact our world through your words/poetry and life experiences. ~ *Lovemore (Sher). lovemorelifestyle.ca*

Colin's poetry is therapeutic. It shows that the Bible is the true Word of God. I am grateful he made me believe in myself again. ~ *Petra James*

Colin was with my family during my dad's final transition and is etched in our memory of my dad's last day on earth. I read his poem at the funeral, and it brought comfort and strength to all of us. He was an Angel sent to be with us on that day. ~ *Charles Jackman*

In *The Soul of a Man,* Colin traces his journey through a difficult period in his life when he lost everything. In those dark moments he found salvation in God's grace and blessings. The book subtitle speaks to its subject content: "A testimony to rising out of darkness to find faith and one's true calling." Colin traces these past years since his soul awakening and shares his insight on living his faith in God's holy grace. ~ *Cheryl Antao-Xavier*

Meet the Author

Colin Jones was born on May 3, 1966, in Kingston, Jamaica. He migrated to Canada at the age of 9 and lived in a low-income housing neighborhood called Regent Park.

Colin has seven siblings, some of whom he knew and the others he did not live with until he arrived in Canada. He also has three beautiful children.

He went through many hardships including a tough divorce. He lost his home, his job and that's when depression began to set in. He began to hang out with the wrong crowd. He went down many different roads of darkness. He suffered anxiety, depression, and PTSD.

He gives back to the community by volunteering at Saint Michael's Hospital and buys food for the homeless when he can. He is a man full of passion and humanity for God's people.

Colin has PSW credentials and a psychology background through University courses. But to him that's not what life is all about. He realized he was seeking the wrong things in life, and it brought him to some dark days where he felt his life was worth nothing. He felt unworthy and this made him want to hurt himself. He went on this journey of darkness to some places that he never thought he would go—a place where you are told when it's shower time, when to eat and when to go to bed.

"I call this place my upper room where God found me and blessed me with one of His greatest gifts—writing His words in poetry," says Colin.

This journey could have killed him, but God preserved him and blessed him and even though he lost a lot of things God gave him back just what he needed—His peace and the love he craved.

This book will take you into the soul of a man. Colin's passion now is to heal God's people with poetry and bring them closer to The One who created everything. So, follow him into his soul and feel the passion in him.